Unspoken Words

Brandi Fulp

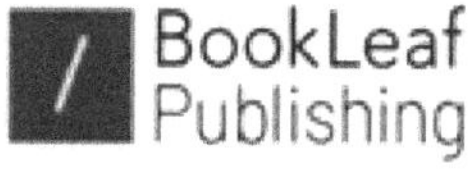

Presentation by *BookLeaf Publishing*

Web: www.bookleafpub.com

E-mail: info@bookleafpub.com

ISBN: 9789357210621

First edition 2022

DEDICATION

I dedicate this book to my family and friends. Thank you for supporting me throughout the years. I love you all!

Have You Ever?

Have you ever felt lost
Not knowing where life is taking you?
Have you ever felt insecure
Not knowing what people are thinking of you?

Have you ever felt sadness
Just surviving through the day?
Have you ever felt regret
From the words you say?

Have you ever felt fear
Thinking that today may be the end?
Have you ever felt anxiety
For no reason to begin?

Have you ever fell asleep
Feeling like today was the best?
Have you ever woken up
Hoping today was like the rest?

Have you ever smiled
But felt depressed inside?
Have you ever kept your composure
Instead of breaking down to cry?

Life is emotional,

And some days could be better.
But just keep positive and write your story
Instead of asking, "Have I ever?"

I Give Up

Cried myself to sleep
Because I had a bad day.
I wish all this negative shit
Would go away.

Broken hearts and broken dreams
Are never meant to be.
But somehow these things
Always happen to me.

Crushed, defeated, frustrated
Tired of facing the day.
But it always seems to get worse
No matter how much I pray.

Getting drunk and getting high
Just to fucking cope.
That's a sign that you've given up
And lost all faith and hope.

College Haiku

Late night studying
Finals week is coming up
I hope I can pass

What should I do now?
This paper's due tomorrow
Can I get this done?

Procrastination
Is what I'm truly good at
Why get a degree?

I need to sleep bad,
Or else I can't go to work
I can't call out sick

Need this done tonight
This mission impossible
Will get done somehow

Healing

My heart is broken.
Loneliness is taking over me.
But I've been telling myself
This wasn't meant to be.

Alcohol and wild nights
Take over my free time.
But when the hangover and pain fades away
I know that I'll be fine.

I'm over crying in the dark
And reflecting what went wrong.
The hurt I felt with you
Is now completely gone.

Things are getting better slowly
And I know I'll be okay soon.
I'm making progress everyday
Because time is healing all my wounds.

Broken Glass

They say, "Words can't bring us down,"
But that is all a lie.
Because the words that are coming from within
me
Take me to a dark place.

Insecurity: a feeling you get from not meeting
the standards of society
A shut-down in your self-esteem.
Feeling like a broken glass collecting dust in a
wooden cabinet,
While the others are expensive China and pretty
antiques.

Tears roll down my cheeks as I look in the
mirror.
My acne is taunting me.
My nerdy glasses block the windows to my
helpless soul,
And my crooked teeth are desperately crying to
be straightened.

My chubby body overflowing in my jeans and
black top

Make me want to starve myself even more than
before.
Maybe I'll skip a meal or two,
Then jog around the block until my body starts
to shake.

My hair is a giant web of brown strands,
Looking like a big tumbleweed rolling through
the desert.
The ends are split, and the whole thing frizzed,
Damaged and tangled like the mess I am.

I despise the reflection staring back.
Thinking what I would look like if I wasn't
broken.
What if I was built to be a little skinnier and
taller?
Would I become a shining star or would I still be
invisible?

The pain that remains from this insecurity will
never be healed.
I'll always feel like an outcast in the world,
And will always critique myself,
Even in the smallest of ways.

No makeup or jewelry can disguise the real me,
Because I'll always be the broken glass.
I guess I'll have to continue living life

As my own worst enemy.

Her Story

This is the story of a girl
Who fell in love real young.
She thought she had found her forever,
But now she's feeling hurt and dumb.

Things started out great
But nothing lasts forever.
After all the time wasted,
She realized she deserved better.

She went on dates and cheated
To fill that emptiness in her heart
Because he stopped believing in her,
Which made her fall apart.

The emotional abuse and manipulation
Fucker her up in the end.
She spent nights crying and wondering if she left
Will she ever love again?

The sex with him became a chore
And the time spent together was a waste.
In the back of her mind she couldn't leave,
She faded to a dark place.

The crying and depression was too much.
It became a daily routine.
The pills she took didn't help.
She just wanted to end everything.

She started looking for sex, drugs and alcohol
In order to feel happy again.
But on the nights she stayed sober,
She wanted her life to end.

Suicide had never crossed her mind
Until this sudden whim.
She was fucked up mentally and emotionally
All because of him.

She constantly prayed and hoped
To the mighty power above.
But none of her prayers were ever answered.
She just wanted to be loved.

But then she met some people
Who pieced her back together.
They showed they cared; they knew her worth,
Her past didn't even matter.

This girl has been through so much
And surprised she's still on Earth.
But through all the trials and tribulations,
She finally knows her worth.

Forever Dreaming

You are always on my mind,
You walk through the hallways of my
unreachable desire.
I can't stop thinking about you.
I get tongue-tied when you're around.
I struggle to find the words to say.
My thoughts are going crazy,
But my mouth is paralyzed in fear.
Why can't I speak?

Why must I be like this?
Every time you say my name,
I feel complete.
I see us walking hand in hand in the fields,
The hot rays of the sun glistening upon us.
You are the best thing that's ever happened to
me.

But that is all a dream.
You don't know who I am.
You don't even notice me.
In reality, I watch you from afar.
I guess I'll just keep dreaming.

Unspoken Words

These words have never been spoken
They've been bottled up inside.
I'm afraid of the emotions
That I no longer can deny.

Can I tell the truth
Without being judged?
Can I tell someone how I really feel
And still receive support and love?

This is it.
All these thoughts are coming out.
The world will now be able to see
What my life is all about.

These poems about my life
Can now be seen and heard.
No more hiding or holding back.
No more unspoken words.

Dear Mom

Dear mom,
I've watched you struggle through the years,
Raising three daughters on your own.
I wondered how you made it look so easy.

I've seen you go through many challenges in life.
But through them all,
You've always had a smile on your face.
You taught me how to be strong.
I've seen you get hurt so much,
But you've always told me,
"God has a better plan."
You taught me to have faith.

There were times I didn't listen,
And we got into some heated arguments.
But in the end I know,
You just wanted what was best for me.

Now that I'm older,
I take all your lectures to heart.
You helped me prepare for the "real world,"
And showed me that life is not easy.

I appreciate and love you so much.

You have raised me to be the best I could be.
You showed me how to be,
The kind of mom I want to be someday.

Just Me

I wish I could say that when I look in the mirror,
I see a Barbie Doll.
A beauty, a model, a shining star,
But that's not me at all.

In reality I see a girl,
With glasses and tons of zits.
Whose self-confidence is torn,
Into tiny little bits.

People tell me that I'm pretty,
And that I'm beautiful and cute.
But I feel that they're all lying,
Because the mirror speaks the truth.

Why can't I just believe,
What these people say?
Why must I criticize myself,
Each and every day?

But I know deep down that people are right,
I really do look okay.
It's just my insecurity and low self-esteem,
That's making me think this way.

I guess I'm overpowered,
By this insecurity.
Because there's nothing wrong with my features
at all.
The problem is just me.

Final Letter

I never told you this,
But you really hurt me.
This didn't work out,
But I felt I did my best.

I was angry and depressed at first,
But I'm finally at peace.
I'm slowly healing day by day,
And realizing my self-worth.

I'm learning independence,
And starting a new journey in life.
I'm seeking what I want and need.
My mind is filled with clarity.

Thank you for being a part of my life,
And for all the memories we had.
I wish you nothing but the best.
I know we'll both be okay.

Only A Dream

Today was the first time,
That you and I got together.
We teased and flirted like we usually do,
Our connection was incredible.

We cuddled on your couch,
And talked about our lives.
Our goals, our hobbies, our daily tasks,
The downfalls we've survived.

Our time together was amazing,
It was a moment of pure bliss.
Before we knew it you and I,
Were engaged in our first kiss.

The chills went through my body,
My heart was pounding fast.
I didn't want to let you go.
I wanted this moment to last.

The alarm clock suddenly went off.
Things were worse than it seemed.
Because everything that just happened,
Was only just a dream.

Thinking, Wishing, Wondering

I'm wishing you were here right now,
Instead of wherever you may be.
I miss you.
My lips don't want to say it,
But my heart does.
Thinking about the memories we had.
The good times and the bad.
I wonder what would have happened,
If we continued on like that?
I always wonder if you're happy,
And I wish you would miss me too.
But I think it would be best,
If we just go on alone.

Aloha Friday Haiku

Today is Friday
This weekend is gonna rock
Lets do something fun

Going to the bar
To have some Tequila shots
Don't talk about work.

Forget the bad times
And let loose tonight
You only live once.

Dear Dad

Dear Dad,
Thank you for all that you've done for me.
We didn't have the best relationship growing up.
I was stubborn and wrong.

I think part of me was still angry,
At the childhood I lived.
I didn't understand it back then,
But now I do.

I remember you always told me "practice makes perfect,"
And it's a motto I still live by today.
You made sure sister and I were taken care of,
Even though I didn't think it.

Things could have been better,
But I like our relationship now.
I'm grateful for you and I am no longer angry.
I love you and appreciate you.

Finding Happiness

Deep down I feel alone,
But I try to see the good.
I try to be positive even though it's hard,
Because I know I really should.

I thought these sexy conversations would help,
But it ended in regret.
The hurt and shame I felt that night,
Was the worst scenario yet.

I ended up making a mistake,
That led to tears the next day.
I felt confused and appalled by it,
Didn't want the night to end that way.

I'm trying to find my happy place,
And not seek it in a man.
It's rough but I know I can be positive.
I know I truly can.

Re-Meeting

When I saw you again,
I felt these mixed emotions.
My anxiety went through the roof,
But I was also glad to see you.

Our conversation was the most genuine it ever
was,
As we laughed and updated each other on life.
Why couldn't our relationship have been like
that?
Why didn't we have that foundation from the
start?

I will always care about you and love you.
Seeing you again made the feelings come back.
We will always have that special connection.
You will always have a special place in my
heart.

I love you.

Ghosted

We started chatting in mid-March,
And we had planned to meet up soon.
We both were going through the same shit,
And we needed a vent session.

You told me at one point you couldn't stop
thinking about me,
And I vented to you about my breakup.
You comforted me and said we should hang out.
And we made plans for the following week.

That night came quickly,
And I waited at the bar.
After two hours I realized,
You weren't going to show up.

You didn't respond to my messages,
And I haven't heard from you since.
Although I've moved on with life,
I'm just extremely bummed you ghosted me.

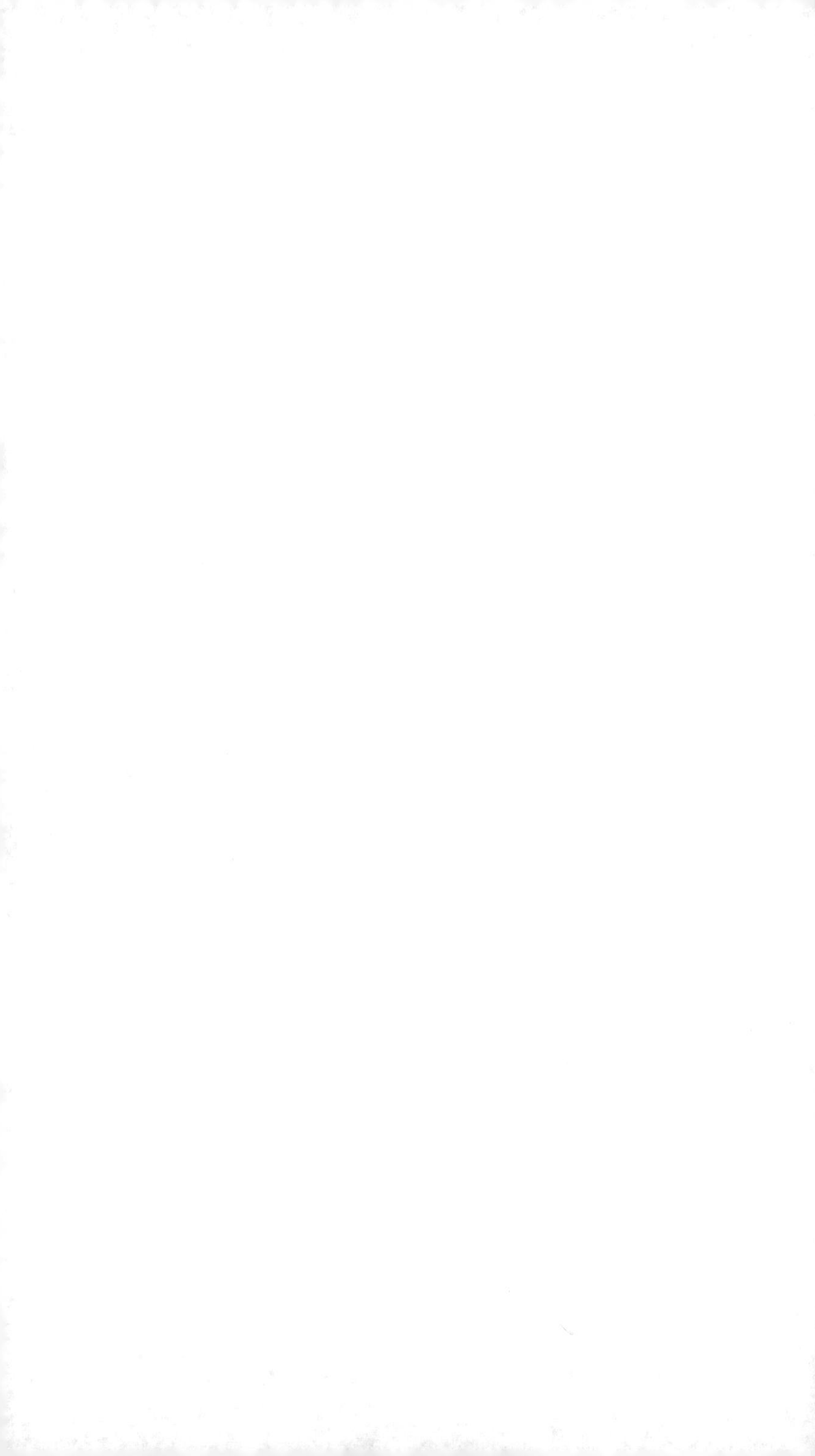

www.ingramcontent.com/pod-product-compliance
Lightning Source LLC
LaVergne TN
LVHW050507210726

843509LV00015BA/3030